D1324043

When I'm Feeling
Kind

Written and illustrated by Trace Moroney

The Five Mile Press

When I'm feeling kind
I feel soft and gentle and caring...
And my heart feels really warm.

When I'm feeling kind
I like to do things that help other people.

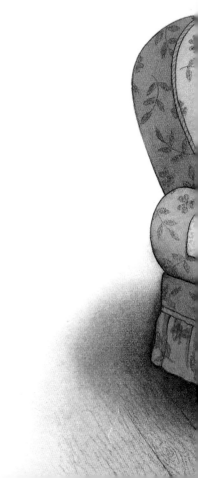

Feeling kind helps me understand
how other people may be feeling.

There are many things
that I like to do
when I feel kind . . .
like help Mum
clean the house,

or *listen*
to a friend
talk about
a problem
they have.

or give a friend a big hug
when he's feeling sad.

Kindness is something I can also
give to *myself.*

Being kind to myself means
liking who I am and being proud
of the things I'm good at . . .

instead of worrying about the things
I'm not so good at!

Being kind to myself means
looking after my body.
I look after it by eating healthy food, exercisi

ery day

and getting lots of sleep!

When I'm feeling kind
I find it easy to be polite and have good manners.
When I ask for something
I always say . . .

please

and when someone gives me something
I always say . . .

thank you

Kindness is something that makes
everyone feel really good . . .
especially me!